Table of Content

Table of Content 1

Chapter 1: An overview of biathlon and its unique blend of skiing and rifle shooting 4

Chapter 2: 7

Origins of biathlon 7

Tracing the sport back to its roots in military training exercises in Scandinavia 10

Chapter 3: 13

Evolution of biathlon as a competitive sport 13

The transition from military training to a recognized Olympic event 16

Chapter 4: 18

Early competitions and athletes in biathlon 18

Profiles of key figures who helped popularize the sport 21

Chapter 5: 24

Biathlon in the Winter Olympics 24

The inclusion of biathlon in the Olympic program and its growth in popularity 27

Chapter 6: 29

Development of biathlon as a sport 29

Improvements in equipment, training methods, and technology 32

Chapter 7: 36

Biathlon disciplines and rules 36

Overview of the various biathlon events and regulations 40

Chapter 8: 43

Biathlon championships and World Cup events 43

The major international competitions in the sport 46

Chapter 9: 49

Biathlon athletes and their impact on the sport 49

Profiles of legendary biathletes and their contributions to the sport 52

Chapter 10: 55

The role of national federations and organizations in biathlon 55

The governance and promotion of biathlon on a global scale 58

Chapter 11: 61

Biathlon as a legacy of military traditions 61

Examining the historical connections between biathlon and military training 65

Chapter 12: 68

Social and cultural impact of biathlon 68

How the sport has influenced society and popular culture 71

Chapter 13: 74

Challenges and controversies in biathlon 74

Addressing issues such as doping, equipment regulations, and gender equality 78

Chapter 14: 80

Future of biathlon as an Olympic sport 80

Potential developments and advancements in the sport 83

Chapter 15: Conclusion.. 86

Reflecting on the evolution of biathlon and its place in the history of winter sports. 86

Chapter 1: An overview of biathlon and its unique blend of skiing and rifle shooting

Biathlon is a unique and fascinating sport that combines two seemingly contrasting activities: skiing and rifle shooting. This combination of endurance and marksmanship has its roots in the military, where soldiers were trained to shoot while on skis. Today, biathlon has evolved into a popular winter sport that is featured in the Winter Olympics and other international competitions.

The sport of biathlon is said to have originated in northern Europe, with early forms of military ski training incorporating rifle shooting. Over time, the focus shifted from military tactics to competitive sport, and biathlon became a popular pastime in countries with a strong winter sports tradition.

The rules of biathlon are relatively simple- athletes race around a cross-country ski course while stopping to shoot at targets set at predetermined distances. Each miss results in a time penalty or a penalty lap, depending on the competition rules. The combination of physical exertion and concentration makes biathlon an incredibly demanding and mentally challenging sport.

One of the most exciting aspects of biathlon is the transition from skiing to shooting. Athletes must lower their heart rate and steady their breathing in order to shoot accurately. This adds an element of strategy and mental fortitude to the sport, making it a captivating spectacle for both participants and spectators.

The equipment used in biathlon is also unique. Athletes must ski with specialized rifles on their backs and carry ammunition for the shooting rounds. The rifles themselves are designed for accuracy and reliability in cold and snowy conditions, with biathletes often using specially adapted sights to aid in target acquisition.

Biathlon has gained a strong following in countries such as Norway, Sweden, and Russia, where it is a part of their national sporting identity. The sport has also gained popularity in countries without a strong tradition of winter sports, thanks in part to its exciting blend of athleticism and marksmanship.

In this chapter, we will explore the history of biathlon, the intricacies of its rules and equipment, and the physical and mental demands it places on its athletes. From its military origins to its current status as an Olympic event, biathlon has a rich and fascinating history that continues to captivate enthusiasts around the world.

Chapter 2:

Origins of biathlon

The sport of biathlon, which combines cross-country skiing and rifle marksmanship, has a history that dates back to the 18th century. Its origins can be traced to Scandinavian countries such as Norway and Sweden, where local militaries utilized a form of skiing and shooting competition as a method of training for soldiers.

The word "biathlon" itself comes from the Greek words "bi" and "athlon," meaning "two" and "sports" respectively, reflecting the two disciplines that make up the sport. While skiing and shooting have been traditional activities in Scandinavian countries for centuries, the combination of the two as a single sport did not take shape until the late 19th and early 20th centuries.

The first recorded biathlon competition took place in Norway in 1767, where participants skied for a distance of 20km while stopping to shoot at targets along the way. This early form of biathlon was known as "ski-grener," and it laid the foundation for the modern sport that we know today.

In the 19th century, the sport began to gain recognition as a military training exercise, with various military units across Europe using it as a way to improve the physical and mental capabilities of their soldiers. The skills required in biathlon, such as endurance, marksmanship, and composure under pressure, made it an ideal training tool for military forces.

As the sport evolved, biathlon competitions became popular across Europe, with the first known civilian biathlon race held in Austria in 1912. However, it wasn't until the mid-20th century that biathlon truly began to take shape as a competitive sport.

In 1924, the first modern Winter Olympics were held in Chamonix, France, and biathlon was included in the program as a demonstration sport. Its success at the Olympics led to the formation of the International Biathlon Union (IBU) in 1948, with the first Biathlon World Championships held in 1958.

The sport continued to grow in popularity, and in 1960, biathlon became an official event at the Winter Olympics in Squaw Valley, California. Since then, it has grown to become one of the most exciting and challenging winter sports, capturing the attention of millions of fans around the world.

Today, biathlon continues to evolve, with advancements in equipment, technology, and training methods pushing the boundaries of what is possible in the sport. From its humble beginnings as a military training exercise to its modern status as an Olympic discipline, biathlon has come a long way, and its journey from military origins to Olympic glory is a testament to the enduring appeal and excitement of this unique sport.

Tracing the sport back to its roots in military training exercises in Scandinavia

Tracing the roots of biathlon back to its origins in military training exercises in Scandinavia is a fascinating journey that provides insight into the rich history of this exhilarating sport. The combination of cross-country skiing and rifle marksmanship that defines biathlon can be traced back to the practical skills and physical endurance required of military troops in the harsh winter conditions of Northern Europe.

The origins of biathlon can be traced as far back as the 18th century, where it emerged as a way for Scandinavian soldiers to maintain their fitness and hunting skills during the long, harsh winters. In countries like Norway, Sweden, and Finland, where snow and ice cover the landscape for much of the year, skiing was a practical and efficient means of transportation, and soldiers were trained to ski and shoot in case of enemy attack. This combination of skiing and marksmanship was not only useful for military purposes, but also provided an effective way for soldiers to stay in prime physical condition during the long, dark winter months.

As the sport evolved, the Norwegian military developed the first known biathlon competition in 1767, known as the "military patrol." This early form of the sport involved a team of soldiers skiing through difficult terrain with rifles, and the competition served as both a means of training and a display of military prowess. Over time, the sport gained popularity and spread to other parts of Scandinavia, eventually taking on the more modern form of individual and relay races that we see in the Olympic Games today.

The skills developed through the military roots of the sport are still evident in the modern-day biathlon. The physical demands of skiing long distances and then controlling breathing and heart rate in order to shoot accurately require a unique combination of endurance, strength, and mental focus, all of which were necessary for soldiers on the battlefield.

It is clear that the military origins of biathlon have left a lasting imprint on the sport, and it is important to understand this heritage in order to fully appreciate the unique combination of athleticism and marksmanship that defines biathlon today. By tracing the sport back to its Scandinavian roots, we can gain a greater appreciation for the rich history and tradition that has shaped biathlon into the thrilling and demanding sport that it is today.

Chapter 3:

Evolution of biathlon as a competitive sport

Biathlon has a rich and fascinating history that has evolved over centuries to become the popular competitive sport that it is today. From its origins in military training to its inclusion in the Winter Olympics, the biathlon has undergone significant changes and innovations.

The sport of biathlon has its roots in the hunting and survival skills of indigenous peoples, particularly those living in the Arctic regions of Scandinavia and Russia. These early inhabitants relied on skis and weapons for transportation and hunting, and the combination of skiing and shooting became a practical and efficient means of survival. As settlements and civilizations developed, these skills were adapted for military use, with troops using skis and firearms for reconnaissance and defensive purposes.

The competitive aspect of biathlon emerged in Scandinavia in the 18th century, with the first recorded biathlon competition held in Norway in 1767. The modern sport as we know it today, however, began to take shape in the early 20th century with the establishment of the first biathlon club in Norway in 1924. This marked the beginning of organized biathlon competitions, and the sport steadily gained popularity in Europe.

The biathlon's competitive format continued to develop, and in 1958, the Union Internationale de Pentathlon Moderne et Biathlon (UIPMB) was founded as the international governing body for the sport. The UIPMB established standardized rules and regulations for biathlon competitions, and in 1960, the sport made its Olympic debut at the Winter Games in Squaw Valley, California.

Since its inclusion in the Olympics, biathlon has continued to evolve and grow in popularity. The sport has seen significant technological advances, including improvements in ski and rifle design, as well as the introduction of electronic targets and timing systems.

These advancements have enhanced the competitiveness and precision of the sport, while also attracting a wider audience.

The evolution of biathlon has also led to the establishment of various international competitions, including the Biathlon World Championships and the Biathlon World Cup.

In recent years, biathlon has continued to thrive as a competitive sport, with a growing number of participants and spectators around the world. The sport's unique combination of physical endurance, marksmanship, and strategy has captured the interest of fans and athletes alike, and biathlon's future as a competitive sport appears to be bright.

The sport has undergone significant changes and innovations over the years, and its continued growth and success are a testament to its enduring appeal. With its rich history and exciting competitive format, biathlon is sure to remain a thrilling and captivating sport for years to come.

The transition from military training to a recognized Olympic event

The biathlon has a long and fascinating history that began in the snowy and rugged terrain of the Scandinavian countries in the late 18th century. Originally, the biathlon was used as a form of military training, combining the skills of skiing and shooting to enhance the physical and mental capabilities of soldiers. Over time, the biathlon evolved into a popular sport, gaining recognition and popularity across the world.

The transition from a military training exercise to a recognized Olympic event was a significant milestone in the history of the biathlon. The sport officially made its debut in the Winter Olympics in 1960 in Squaw Valley, United States as a men's event. The first women's biathlon event was introduced in Innsbruck, Austria during the 1976 Winter Olympics.

The inclusion of the biathlon in the Olympics was a testament to its growing popularity as a competitive sport. The physical and mental demands of the sport, combined with the graceful and challenging aspects of cross-country skiing, attracted a dedicated following among athletes and fans alike. The transition to an Olympic event also brought increased resources and funding to the sport, enabling the development of modern equipment, training facilities, and coaching programs.

The recognition of the biathlon as an Olympic event also provided the opportunity for biathletes to compete at the highest level of international competition. The sport has continued to grow in popularity, with countries around the world actively participating in biathlon events and developing talented athletes.

Today, the biathlon has firmly established itself as a thrilling and challenging Olympic sport, showcasing the skill, precision, and endurance of its participants. The transition from its origins as military training to a recognized Olympic event is a testament to the evolution and growth of the biathlon, making it a significant and celebrated part of the Winter Olympics.

Chapter 4:

Early competitions and athletes in biathlon

From its military origins to its progression into an Olympic event, the biathlon has a rich history that is marked by the skill and determination of its athletes.

The sport of biathlon has its roots in the hunting and survival skills of Northern European countries, where the ability to ski and shoot were essential for surviving in the harsh winter conditions. These skills were eventually adapted for military use, with soldiers in countries such as Norway, Sweden, and Russia using skiing and marksmanship as part of their training.

The first organized biathlon competition took place in Norway in 1767, with soldiers from different regiments competing against each other in a ski race with shooting stops along the way. This laid the foundation for the modern biathlon, which has evolved to include various formats such as sprint, pursuit, individual, and relay races.

Early biathlon athletes were often military personnel who excelled in skiing and marksmanship. One notable early competitor was Ole Einar Bjørndalen, who hails from Norway and is considered one of the greatest biathletes of all time.

Other notable early athletes include Antje Misersky from Germany, who won multiple medals at the World Championships in the 1980s, and Sergei Tchepikov from Russia, who dominated the sport in the early 2000s.

As the sport gained popularity, more countries began developing biathlon programs, and the competition became increasingly fierce. Athletes from traditionally non-biathlon nations such as France, Italy, and the United States began to emerge as strong contenders on the world stage.

The early development of biathlon as a competitive sport laid the groundwork for its eventual inclusion in the Winter Olympics. The sport made its Olympic debut in 1960 and has since become a highlight of the games, attracting athletes from all over the world to compete for glory on the international stage.

From its humble beginnings as a military training exercise to its status as a celebrated Olympic event, biathlon has come a long way thanks to the dedication and talent of its early competitors. Their legacy continues to inspire a new generation of athletes to push the boundaries of the sport and strive for excellence on the global stage.

Profiles of key figures who helped popularize the sport

The biathlon is a sport that combines cross-country skiing and rifle shooting. It has origins in military training exercises and has evolved into a highly competitive Olympic sport. Over the years, several key figures have played a crucial role in popularizing and promoting the sport at both the national and international levels. In this book, we profile some of the most influential figures in the biathlon world, whose contributions have led to the sport's rise to Olympic glory.

1. Ole Einar Bjørndalen- Known as the "King of Biathlon," Ole Einar Bjørndalen is one of the most successful biathletes in history. His success on the world stage has played a significant role in raising the profile of biathlon as a sport, particularly in Norway and across Scandinavia.

2. Magdalena Forsberg- Hailing from Sweden, Magdalena Forsberg is widely regarded as one of the greatest female biathletes of all time. Her competitive

spirit and exceptional athletic abilities have inspired a new generation of biathletes, contributing to the global appeal of the sport.

3. Wilhelm Gruhn- As a coach, Wilhelm Gruhn has played an instrumental role in advancing the sport of biathlon. His expertise and innovative training methods have helped develop successful biathletes from Germany, who have gone on to achieve notable success on the international stage. Gruhn's influence as a coach has not only elevated the performance of German biathletes, but has also contributed to the sport's growth and professionalism worldwide.

4. Darya Domracheva- Hailing from Belarus, Darya Domracheva has left an indelible mark on the sport of biathlon. With a record-breaking Olympic gold medal haul and multiple World Championship victories, Domracheva has emerged as a trailblazing figure in the biathlon world. Her accomplishments have not only elevated the visibility of biathlon in Belarus, but have also heightened global interest in the sport, particularly in Eastern Europe.

5. Raphaël Poirée- A former French biathlete, Raphaël Poirée's impact on the sport extends beyond his impressive athletic achievements. Poirée's charismatic personality and sporting prowess have

helped popularize biathlon in France, paving the way for the sport to gain prominence in the country. As an ambassador for biathlon, Poirée has inspired countless individuals to pursue the sport, contributing to its continued growth and success.

These key figures, among many others, have played significant roles in popularizing the sport of biathlon and elevating its status to one of Olympic glory. Through their exceptional talent, dedication, and influence, they have forged legacies that have left enduring impacts on the biathlon world, inspiring generations of athletes and fans alike.

Chapter 5:

Biathlon in the Winter Olympics

The biathlon is a unique and challenging sport that combines two disciplines: cross-country skiing and rifle shooting. It has a rich history that dates back to the 18th century and has its origins in the military. Biathlon made its Olympic debut in the 1960 Winter Olympics in Squaw Valley, USA. Since then, it has been a popular event at the Winter Games, attracting athletes from around the world.

The biathlon event in the Winter Olympics consists of several different races, including the individual, sprint, pursuit, mass start, and relay races. The individual race is the longest and most grueling, with athletes skiing a certain distance and shooting at targets from a prone and standing position. The sprint race is shorter, with athletes completing a faster, more intense course with two shooting rounds. The pursuit combines the results of the sprint race to determine the starting order, creating an exciting dash to the finish line. The mass start race sees all athletes starting at the same time, creating a thrilling spectacle for spectators. Finally, the relay race involves a team of four athletes, with each member completing a skiing leg and shooting at targets before passing the baton to the next racer.

The biathlon requires a unique blend of physical and mental attributes. Athletes need excellent endurance, strength, and speed to navigate the cross-country skiing portion of the event. They must also possess great marksmanship skills and the ability to stay calm under pressure when shooting at targets. The combination of skiing and shooting creates a dynamic and demanding competition that truly tests the limits of an athlete's abilities.

Over the years, biathlon has produced some extraordinary Olympic moments. Athletes like Ole Einar Bjørndalen, Magdalena Forsberg, and Martin Fourcade have become legends of the sport, dominating the Olympic stage with their skill and determination. The unpredictable nature of biathlon, with its ever-changing shooting conditions and ski tracks, has made for thrilling races and dramatic finishes at the Winter Games.

The biathlon has also evolved and modernized over the years, with improvements in equipment, training methods, and technology. The introduction of electronic targets and tracking systems has enhanced the accuracy and fairness of the sport, while advancements in ski technology and training have allowed athletes to push the boundaries of their physical capabilities.

Its unique combination of cross-country skiing and rifle shooting has provided thrilling moments and unforgettable performances throughout its history. As the sport continues to grow and evolve, it remains an essential part of the Winter Games, captivating audiences with its blend of athleticism, strategy, and drama.

The inclusion of biathlon in the Olympic program and its growth in popularity

Biathlon had humble military origins, but today, it has gained popularity as an Olympic sport that blends incredible endurance and precision shooting. The sport's inclusion in the Olympic program has played a significant role in its growth, allowing it to reach larger audiences and gain recognition globally.

One of the most captivating aspects of biathlon is its rich roots in military and hunting traditions. The sport's origins can be traced back to the northern European countries, where it was developed as a means of training and survival for soldiers and hunters. Naturally, the combination of skiing and shooting was a practical and necessary skill in those times, but over the years, it evolved into a competitive sport that demands remarkable physical and mental abilities.

The book delves into the transformation of biathlon from a survival skill to a high-level Olympic sport. It examines the efforts and contributions of key individuals and organizations in shaping biathlon's rules, competitions, and equipment. Furthermore, the narrative explores the impact of biathlon's inclusion in the Olympic program and its subsequent rise in popularity. The exposure brought by the Olympics has led to increased interest in biathlon, generating more opportunities for competitions, sponsorships, and overall growth of the sport.

The growth of biathlon's popularity is also reflected in the expansion of its fan base and participation globally. The book offers insights into the different countries and regions where biathlon has gained a strong following, as well as the various events and competitions that have attracted athletes from around the world. It also showcases the efforts to promote biathlon to newer generations, ensuring that the sport continues to thrive and evolve in the future.

By highlighting its fascinating history, evolution, and global appeal, the book offers a compelling narrative for both enthusiasts and newcomers to biathlon alike. Whether you're a seasoned fan of the sport or just discovering it for the first time, this book is a valuable resource that celebrates the enduring legacy and future potential of biathlon.

Chapter 6:

Development of biathlon as a sport

Biathlon, a sport that combines the disciplines of cross-country skiing and rifle shooting, has a long and unique history that dates back to its military origins.

The sport of biathlon has its origins in the use of skis and rifles for military purposes. In fact, the word "biathlon" comes from the Greek word for "two tests" or "two contests. " Ski warfare has been a part of the military tradition in Scandinavia for centuries, and it was in Norway that the first modern biathlon competition took place in 1767. The sport grew in popularity in Scandinavia and other European countries, and biathlon competitions and events soon spread across the globe.

The early development of biathlon as a competitive sport was largely influenced by its military origins, and the first modern biathlon competitions included military competitors. However, as the sport continued to grow in popularity, it became more mainstream and civilian athletes began to participate in biathlon events as well.

In the early 20th century, the International Biathlon Union (IBU) was formed to govern and regulate the sport of biathlon. The IBU established rules and regulations for biathlon competitions and worked to standardize the sport on an international level. These efforts helped to codify the rules of biathlon and establish a competitive framework that is still in place today.

One of the most significant developments in the history of biathlon was its inclusion in the Winter Olympics. Biathlon made its Olympic debut at the 1960 Winter Games in Squaw Valley, California, and it has been a regular event ever since. The inclusion of biathlon in the Olympics helped to further popularize the sport and attract new participants and fans from around the world.

In recent years, biathlon has continued to evolve and develop as a sport. Advances in equipment and technology have led to improvements in ski design, rifle accuracy, and training methods, making the sport faster and more competitive than ever before. The growing popularity of biathlon has also led to an increase in the number of international competitions and events, including the Biathlon World Cup and the Biathlon World Championships.

The sport has come a long way since its early days, and it continues to grow and evolve as an exciting and challenging athletic competition. With its unique combination of skiing and shooting, biathlon remains a popular and respected sport with a rich history and a promising future.

Improvements in equipment, training methods, and technology

As biathlon has become more popular and competitive, athletes and coaches have sought to gain any advantage they can in terms of preparation, equipment, and performance. This has led to major developments in all areas of the sport, from the rifles used by athletes to the methods by which they train, to the technology that is now used to enhance their performance.

One of the most notable improvements in biathlon equipment has been the development of more advanced rifles. Modern biathlon rifles are highly sophisticated pieces of equipment, designed to be lightweight, accurate, and reliable in a variety of conditions. These rifles are usually . 22 caliber, allowing for a quick and accurate shot without excessive recoil. Furthermore, many of these rifles are now equipped with electronic or digital sighting systems, giving athletes greater precision when aiming at the small targets in the biathlon shooting range. Additionally, advancements in materials and manufacturing processes have greatly improved the durability and reliability of biathlon rifles, allowing athletes to trust in their equipment under the most demanding circumstances. These improvements have made the rifles used in biathlon more accurate and reliable than ever before, allowing athletes to focus on their shooting without worrying about the functionality of their equipment.

The training methods employed by biathletes have also evolved significantly in recent years. As the sport has become more competitive, athletes have sought to find the most effective and efficient ways to develop their fitness, stamina, and shooting abilities. This has led to the development of new training programs that are specifically tailored to the unique demands of biathlon. These programs often focus on a combination of endurance, strength, and shooting accuracy, requiring athletes to develop a high level of fitness and technical skills. In addition, the use of technology and data analysis has become increasingly important in biathlon training, with athletes and coaches using tools such as heart rate monitors, GPS tracking devices, and video analysis to optimize their training and improve performance. This integration of technology into biathlon training has provided athletes with new tools for monitoring and improving their fitness and shooting abilities, leading to more effective and streamlined training programs.

Advancements in technology have also played a significant role in improving the overall experience of biathlon. For example, the introduction of electronic targets in biathlon shooting ranges has revolutionized the sport by providing instant and accurate feedback to athletes and spectators. These targets are equipped with sensors that detect when a shot has been fired, immediately displaying the result on a digital screen. This has not only made the competition more transparent and exciting, but has also allowed athletes to track their shooting performance with greater precision, gaining valuable insights that can be used to make adjustments in real time.

Athletes now have access to more sophisticated and reliable equipment, as well as more efficient and effective training programs, leading to better performance on the track and in the shooting range. The integration of technology has also enhanced the overall experience of biathlon, allowing for greater precision, fairness, and excitement in the sport. As biathlon continues to grow in popularity and level of competition, it is likely that further advancements in equipment, training methods, and technology will continue to drive the sport forward.

Chapter 7:

Biathlon disciplines and rules

Biathlon has a long and rich history as a winter sport, originating from the military skills of skiing and shooting. Today, it has evolved into an exciting Olympic discipline that combines the endurance of cross-country skiing with the precision and focus of rifle marksmanship. In this section, we will explore the various disciplines and rules of biathlon.

The biathlon event consists of several different disciplines, each with its own rules and regulations. The most common and well-known discipline is the individual event, where athletes compete in a series of shooting rounds interspersed with laps of skiing. The distance of the skiing laps and the number of shooting rounds vary depending on the specific competition, but the format generally remains the same. Athletes are required to ski a certain distance, usually ranging from 10 to 20 kilometers, with shooting stops at designated ranges.

The shooting component of biathlon is divided into two positions: prone and standing. In the prone position, athletes must shoot at a target 50 meters away, and in the standing position, they must shoot at the same distance. The targets are 45mm in diameter for the prone position and 115mm for the standing position. Athletes are required to hit as many targets as possible within a certain number of shots, and penalties are incurred for each missed target. These penalties typically come in the form of extra skiing laps or added time to the athlete's overall race time.

Another popular discipline in biathlon is the sprint event, which is a shorter and more intense version of the individual event. The skiing distance is usually around 10 kilometers, and the number of shooting rounds is reduced to two, one in the prone position and one in the standing position. The sprint event is known for its fast-paced and exciting nature, with athletes pushing their physical and mental limits to complete the race in the fastest time.

In addition to the individual and sprint events, biathlon also features a pursuit event, a mass start event, and a relay event. Each of these disciplines has its own unique set of rules and challenges, but they all incorporate the fundamental skills of skiing and shooting that define biathlon as a sport.

As for the rules of biathlon, athletes are subject to strict guidelines regarding equipment, conduct, and fair play. Rifles must meet specific criteria for weight, length, and caliber, and ski equipment must adhere to certain standards for size and shape. Athletes are also required to conduct themselves in a professional and sportsmanlike manner, adhering to the ethical and anti-doping regulations set forth by the International Biathlon Union (IBU) and the Olympic Committee.

Overall, the disciplines and rules of biathlon are integral to the sport's identity and its place in the Olympic landscape. From the individual event to the relay event, biathlon offers a unique blend of athleticism, precision, and strategy that continues to captivate audiences around the world. Whether you're a seasoned biathlon enthusiast or new to the sport, understanding the various disciplines and rules of biathlon adds depth and appreciation to this truly remarkable winter sport.

Overview of the various biathlon events and regulations

The biathlon is a challenging winter sport that combines cross-country skiing and precision rifle shooting. The roots of the biathlon can be traced back to its military origins, where soldiers practiced their marksmanship and skiing skills for combat readiness. Over time, the biathlon has evolved into a popular international sport, with competitions held at the Olympic Games and World Championships.

There are several different biathlon events, each with its own set of regulations and challenges. The most common event is the individual biathlon, where athletes ski a specific distance and then shoot at targets from both standing and prone positions. Each missed target results in a penalty, which can manifest as added time or a penalty loop that the athlete must ski before continuing on the course.

In addition to the individual event, the biathlon also includes sprint, pursuit, mass start, and relay races. The sprint event is a shorter distance race with two shooting stages, while the pursuit event is a longer race that begins with athletes starting based on their finishing times from a previous race. The mass start event involves all athletes racing at once, and the relay event requires teams of four to take turns skiing and shooting.

Regulations for the biathlon events cover a wide range of aspects, including equipment, course design, and shooting techniques. Athletes must use specially designed biathlon rifles, and they are required to shoot from a designated shooting range to ensure safety and fairness. The course layout includes various terrain features such as uphill and downhill sections, as well as challenging turns and obstacles.

Shooting accuracy is an essential component of the biathlon, and athletes must employ a combination of physical and mental skills to manage their heart rate and breathing while aiming at targets. The pressure of shooting under time constraints and the physical demands of skiing at high speeds over varying terrain make the biathlon a uniquely demanding sport.

Overall, the biathlon offers a compelling blend of athleticism and marksmanship, with a rich history and a deep set of regulations that govern its various events. Athletes from around the world compete in this challenging sport, showcasing their skills and dedication in pursuit of Olympic glory.

Chapter 8:

Biathlon championships and World Cup events

The biathlon world championships are held annually and feature a variety of events including sprint, pursuit, individual, mass start, and relay races. These championships are highly anticipated by both athletes and fans, as they provide an opportunity to witness the best in the sport compete at the highest level.

In addition to the world championships, the biathlon World Cup circuit is a major highlight of the biathlon season. The World Cup events take place throughout the winter months and consist of a series of races held at different venues across Europe and North America. The overall winner of the World Cup is determined by a points system based on the athletes' performances in the individual races.

The World Cup events are a showcase of the sport's top talent, with athletes from countries such as Norway, Russia, Germany, and France dominating the competition. The races feature a combination of both skiing and shooting, requiring athletes to possess exceptional physical endurance and marksmanship skills.

One of the most renowned events on the biathlon World Cup circuit is the Holmenkollen Ski Festival in Oslo, Norway. The festival is held annually and includes a series of biathlon competitions, as well as other winter sports events. The Holmenkollen Ski Festival is a highlight of the biathlon season and attracts thousands of spectators from around the world.

The biathlon world championships and World Cup events are not only about competition; they also play a crucial role in promoting the sport and inspiring the next generation of biathletes. By showcasing the skill and athleticism of the top athletes in the sport, these events help to increase the visibility of biathlon and attract new fans and participants.

Ultimately, the biathlon world championships and World Cup events are a celebration of the sport and its athletes, highlighting the incredible dedication and talent that define biathlon. These competitions provide a platform for the best in the sport to showcase their skills, while also inspiring and entertaining fans around the world.

The major international competitions in the sport

The Winter Olympics is the pinnacle of biathlon competition, with athletes from around the world competing for gold, silver, and bronze medals. The biathlon has been a regular event at the Winter Olympics since the 1960 Games in Squaw Valley, USA. There are a total of 11 biathlon events at the Winter Olympics, including individual, sprint, pursuit, mass start, and relay races for both men and women. Athletes must demonstrate precision marksmanship while also managing the physical demands of cross-country skiing, making the biathlon one of the most challenging and exciting events at the Winter Olympics.

The Biathlon World Championships are held annually and feature individual, sprint, pursuit, mass start, and team relay races for both men and women. The Biathlon World Championships attract the top biathletes from around the world and serve as an important qualification event for the Winter Olympics.

The first Biathlon World Championships were held in 1958 in Austria, and since then, the event has grown in prestige and international participation.

The Biathlon World Cup is a series of competitions held throughout the winter season, with events taking place in various countries across Europe and North America. The Biathlon World Cup is the premier biathlon circuit and features individual, sprint, pursuit, and mass start races for both men and women. Athletes earn points based on their performance in each race, and the overall winners of the World Cup are awarded the prestigious crystal globes. The Biathlon World Cup is highly competitive, with top athletes from Norway, Germany, France, and Russia consistently battling for supremacy on the circuit.

In addition to these major international competitions, there are also regional and national biathlon events held in countries around the world. These competitions serve as important stepping stones for young biathletes looking to develop their skills and compete at the highest levels of the sport.

Overall, the biathlon is a thrilling and challenging sport that combines the physical endurance of cross-country skiing with the precision and focus of rifle marksmanship.

Chapter 9:

Biathlon athletes and their impact on the sport

Biathlon, a winter sport that combines cross-country skiing and rifle shooting, has a rich history that dates back to the 18th century when it was used as a military training exercise in Norway. Since then, the sport has evolved and gained popularity around the world, with athletes competing in a range of international events, encompassing the Winter Olympics, World Championships, and the Biathlon World Cup.

Biathlon athletes are a unique breed of sportspeople, requiring a rare combination of physical fitness, endurance, and marksmanship skills. The demands of the sport are particularly rigorous, as athletes must possess the ability to ski long distances at high speeds, while also maintaining the composure and precision required for shooting accurately at a range.

As a result, Biathlon athletes have a significant impact on the sport. Their commitment and dedication to training and competition push the boundaries of what is physically and mentally achievable. Their achievements continually contribute to the broader evolution and popularity of Biathlon, inspiring a new generation of aspiring athletes to take up the sport.

Moreover, Biathlon athletes are often the faces of their respective countries at international competitions, competing at the highest level and showcasing the global appeal of the sport. Their performances not only bring recognition to themselves and their teams but also serve to ignite passion and interest in Biathlon among audiences worldwide.

The impact of Biathlon athletes also extends beyond the competitive arena. Many athletes are admirable role models and ambassadors for the sport, using their platforms to raise awareness about the sport and to promote its values of discipline, determination, and sportsmanship.

On a competitive level, the performances of Biathlon athletes have significantly raised the standard of the sport, with advancements in training techniques, equipment, and overall athleticism. This has led to increased competitiveness and excitement in Biathlon events, allowing the sport to maintain its status as a thrilling and high-profile discipline.

Additionally, the success of Biathlon athletes has helped to secure the sport's future and attract sponsorship and funding, ensuring it continues to thrive and grow in popularity on the international stage.

Overall, the impact of Biathlon athletes on the sport is undeniable. Their passion, skill, and dedication have elevated the sport to new levels of recognition and planted seeds of inspiration in individuals across the globe. They have acted as key drivers in the constant evolution and rise in popularity of Biathlon, ensuring its position as an enduring and celebrated sport on the international stage.

Profiles of legendary biathletes and their contributions to the sport

Biathlon as a sport has a rich history, filled with the contributions of legendary biathletes who have left a lasting imprint on the sport. These athletes have not only achieved remarkable success and accolades in their careers, but have also shaped the modern landscape of biathlon through their dedication, skill, and passion.

One of the most prominent figures in the history of biathlon is Ole Einar Bjørndalen, often referred to as the "King of Biathlon. " Hailing from Norway, Bjørndalen has an impressive collection of Olympic and World Championship medals, and is widely regarded as one of the greatest biathletes of all time. His meticulous training regimen and unwavering focus made him a dominant force on the biathlon scene for well over a decade. His impact on the sport can be seen in the way he popularized biathlon in Norway and inspired countless young athletes to pursue the sport.

Another key figure in the world of biathlon is Magdalena Forsberg, a Swedish biathlete who dominated the women's circuit in the late 1990s and early 2000s. Forsberg's exceptional shooting accuracy and remarkable skiing ability made her a formidable competitor, and she set a record for the most consecutive World Cup victories in biathlon. Her influence extended beyond the world of competitive biathlon, as she played a pivotal role in raising the profile of the sport in Sweden and inspiring a new generation of biathletes.

These legendary biathletes have made indelible marks on the sport, not only through their athletic achievements, but also through their dedication to growing and promoting biathlon. Their contributions have helped to elevate biathlon to the global stage, and their legacies continue to inspire current and future generations of biathletes.

As biathlon continues to evolve and thrive, the influence of these legendary figures remains profound, serving as a testament to the enduring power and legacy of their contributions to the sport. Their stories, accomplishments, and impact on biathlon are a testament to the enduring legacy of these legendary biathletes in shaping the sport of biathlon.

Chapter 10:

The role of national federations and organizations in biathlon

These organizations are responsible for organizing and promoting biathlon events, developing talent at the grassroots level, and ensuring that athletes have the resources and support they need to compete at the highest level.

National federations are typically responsible for overseeing the sport of biathlon within their respective countries. They work closely with government bodies, sports organizations, and other stakeholders to ensure that biathletes have the infrastructure, facilities, and financial support they need to train and compete. National federations also play a key role in setting standards for coaching, officiating, and athlete development, as well as organizing national competitions and training camps.

In addition to national federations, there are also a number of international organizations that play a key role in the development and promotion of biathlon. The International Biathlon Union (IBU) is the global governing body for the sport, responsible for organizing international competitions, setting the rules and regulations, and promoting the sport on the world stage. The IBU also works closely with national federations to ensure that biathletes from around the world have the opportunity to compete at the highest level.

National federations and organizations also play a crucial role in promoting the values of the sport, including fair play, sportsmanship, and respect for the environment. They work to ensure that the tradition and culture of biathlon are upheld, while also promoting the sport to new generations of athletes and fans.

Through their efforts, biathlon has become a popular and respected sport that is enjoyed by millions of athletes and fans around the world.

The governance and promotion of biathlon on a global scale

Biathlon, a sport that combines the thrill of cross-country skiing with the precision of marksmanship, has a rich and varied history.

At the global level, the International Biathlon Union (IBU) is the governing body for the sport of biathlon. Founded in 1948, the IBU is responsible for establishing and enforcing the rules and regulations of biathlon competitions, as well as promoting the sport around the world. The IBU is also in charge of organizing major events such as the Biathlon World Championships and the Biathlon World Cup, which are the pinnacle of competition in the sport.

One of the key functions of the IBU is to collaborate with national biathlon federations to promote the sport at the grassroots level. This includes developing programs and initiatives to introduce biathlon to new participants, particularly in countries where the sport is less established. By working closely with national federations, the IBU can help to ensure that biathlon continues to grow and thrive, attracting a new generation of athletes and fans.

In addition to the work of the IBU, the promotion of biathlon on a global scale also involves collaboration with other international sports organizations, such as the International Olympic Committee (IOC) and the International Ski Federation (FIS). As biathlon is a winter sport that is closely related to cross-country skiing, it is important for the sport to have a strong presence within the wider winter sports community. This can help to attract funding, media coverage, and commercial partnerships, all of which are essential for the long-term success of the sport.

This means working to address barriers to participation, such as the cost of equipment and facilities, and promoting diversity and equality within the sport. By taking a proactive approach to these issues, the IBU and other stakeholders can help to create a more vibrant and inclusive biathlon community, which in turn can help to attract more participants and fans to the sport.

By working together to promote the sport and ensure its long-term success, these stakeholders can help to secure a bright future for biathlon, both at the grassroots level and on the world stage.

Chapter 11:

Biathlon as a legacy of military traditions

The sport of biathlon has a rich and distinct origin directly rooted in military traditions. Its history can be traced back to the early 19th century when the military forces of Norway, Finland, and Sweden developed skiing and shooting as a means of training and survival in harsh winter environments. These military traditions laid the foundation for what would become the modern biathlon, a sport that combines elements of cross-country skiing and rifle marksmanship.

One of the earliest known military uses of skiing and shooting was by the Norwegian military during the 18th century. The Norwegian army utilized skiing as a means of transportation and combat in the snowy and mountainous terrain of the country. As a result, ski marksmanship became an essential skill for Norwegian soldiers, and they would often organize skiing competitions that included shooting as part of their training exercises.

Similarly, in Finland, the military also recognized the value of skiing and marksmanship in winter warfare. The Finnish military developed the concept of "military patrol," a team event that combined skiing, rifle shooting, and cross-country running. This military patrol, which later evolved into the biathlon, was first introduced as a competitive sport at the 1924 Winter Olympics in Chamonix, France.

Sweden also played a significant role in the development of the biathlon as a military tradition. The Swedish army utilized skiing and marksmanship in its military training and developed specialized units known as "ski troops" or "huntsmen companies" to operate in winter conditions. These units were trained to ski long distances while carrying weapons and supplies and were also skilled marksmen.

The influence of these military traditions on the sport of biathlon is evident in the structure and rules of the modern biathlon competitions. Athletes must ski over varying distances and terrains, stopping at designated shooting ranges to demonstrate their marksmanship under intense physical exertion. This combination of high-intensity skiing and precision shooting reflects the skills and training required of soldiers in winter warfare.

The legacy of military traditions in the sport of biathlon extends beyond its origins. Many biathletes have come from military backgrounds, bringing with them the discipline, focus, and marksmanship skills honed in military training. Some athletes even continue to serve in their respective military forces while competing at the highest level in biathlon competitions, showcasing the strong connection between the sport and its military roots.

In addition to its military origins, biathlon has also maintained a strong presence in military competitions and training exercises. The sport is regularly featured in the military world championships and is used as a means of improving soldier's physical fitness, marksmanship, and tactical skills. The incorporation of biathlon into military training demonstrates its continued relevance as a practical and challenging winter sport that has deep ties to military traditions.

Overall, the legacy of military traditions in biathlon is evident in its origins, structure, and the athletes who compete in the sport. The military forces of Norway, Finland, and Sweden played a pivotal role in the development of skiing and shooting as essential skills for soldiers, laying the groundwork for what would become the modern biathlon. This rich heritage continues to shape and influence the sport, emphasizing the enduring connection between biathlon and its military roots.

Examining the historical connections between biathlon and military training

Biathlon, derived from the Greek word for "two contests", has a long and storied history closely tied to military training. The sport, which combines cross-country skiing and rifle shooting, has its origins in the survival skills practiced by prehistoric hunters and later evolved into a critical component of military training in Europe.

The roots of biathlon can be traced back to the early days of hunting, when the skill of skiing was essential for hunters to cover large distances in pursuit of prey. As societies became more organized, the ability to ski and shoot accurately became an important part of warfare. In countries with harsh winter climates, such as Scandinavia and Russia, skiing and shooting were crucial skills for defending territory and conducting military operations.

During the 18th and 19th centuries, military units across Europe began to formalize these skills into organized training programs. Military ski patrols were established, tasked with traversing intricate and challenging terrain while maintaining sharpshooting skills. These elite units played a vital role in reconnaissance, guerrilla warfare, and other specialized operations.

The development of modern biathlon as a sport can be directly traced to the efforts of the Norwegian military. In the late 19th century, the Norwegian military organized ski competitions that included marksmanship as a way to keep soldiers fit and combat-ready during peacetime. These competitions, known as "military patrol races", laid the groundwork for the biathlon events we see today.

The military roots of biathlon are evident in the equipment used in the sport. Traditional biathlon rifles are modeled after military rifles, with a focus on accuracy, reliability, and ease of use in cold and challenging conditions. Similarly, the skiing techniques utilized in biathlon draw heavily from military ski patrol tactics, with an emphasis on speed, agility, and endurance.

As the sport of biathlon continued to evolve, it garnered interest from civilian populations and eventually made its way into the modern Olympics. Despite its transformation into a mainstream sporting event, the influence of military training remains at the core of biathlon's DNA. Athletes competing in biathlon must possess not only exceptional physical fitness and marksmanship skills but also the mental fortitude and strategic thinking imperative in military operations.

From its origins as a crucial survival skill for prehistoric hunters to its status as a fiercely competitive Olympic sport, biathlon has always been shaped by the demands of militaristic pursuits. Understanding the historical context of biathlon sheds light on its enduring appeal and the unique blend of athleticism and marksmanship that makes it an unparalleled test of skill and endurance.

Chapter 12:

Social and cultural impact of biathlon

Biathlon is a sport that has had a significant social and cultural impact since its military origins. Its unique blend of cross-country skiing and rifle shooting has made it a popular pastime in many countries and has contributed to the development of many winter sports communities.

One of the most significant social impacts of biathlon is its ability to bring people together from different backgrounds. Because the sport requires both physical fitness and marksmanship skills, it appeals to a wide range of athletes who may not have otherwise crossed paths. This has led to the development of a close-knit biathlon community that values teamwork and camaraderie. For many athletes, biathlon is as much about the friendships and connections they make as it is about competing on the course.

Biathlon has also had a cultural impact on many countries where it is popular. In places like Norway, Sweden, and Russia, biathlon is a national pastime with a rich cultural heritage. These countries have produced many of the sport's top athletes and have a deep appreciation for their biathlon traditions. In these countries, biathlon is more than just a sport – it is a part of the national identity.

Another cultural impact of biathlon is its influence on other winter sports. The skills and techniques required for biathlon have helped to shape the development of other sports such as cross-country skiing and rifle shooting. Additionally, biathlon has inspired the creation of new sports that combine elements of both skiing and shooting, further expanding the impact of the sport on winter sports culture.

In recent years, biathlon has also become a popular spectator sport, attracting large crowds and television audiences. This has helped to raise the profile of the sport and has led to increased interest and participation at all levels. As a result, biathlon has become an important part of many communities, contributing to the cultural and social fabric of winter sports.

It has brought people together, influenced national identities, and inspired the development of other sports, while also becoming a popular spectator event. As biathlon continues to grow in popularity, its impact on society and culture is likely to continue to expand.

How the sport has influenced society and popular culture

The sport of biathlon has undeniably had a profound influence on both society and popular culture since its inception as a military training exercise. Its unique combination of cross-country skiing and precision rifle shooting has not only captivated sports enthusiasts and athletes, but has also contributed to a broader discussion about the intersection of athleticism, marksmanship, and mental fortitude.

Society has been influenced by the sport of biathlon in numerous ways, both on and off the range. Biathletes have served as prominent figures in military and civilian leadership, utilizing their dedication, discipline, and focus to inspire others in their professional and personal lives. The sport has also fostered a sense of national pride and community in countries with strong biathlon traditions, as athletes compete on the world stage and bring home medals for their respective nations.

In popular culture, biathlon has garnered a dedicated following and has been featured in various forms of media, including films, television shows, and documentaries. The intense competition and physical prowess required to excel in the sport have made biathlon a compelling subject for filmmakers and writers, contributing to its increased visibility and influence in the public consciousness.

The athletic prowess demonstrated by biathletes and the mental and physical challenges of the sport have also captured the imagination of artists and musicians, who have drawn inspiration from the ethos and imagery of biathlon. Its unique marriage of physical strength and precision shooting has made biathlon a symbol of dedication, perseverance, and excellence in the eyes of many creatives.

Public interest in biathlon has also led to the development of biathlon-themed merchandise, events, and experiences, further cementing its influence in popular culture. From biathlon-themed fashion lines to recreational shooting ranges that offer a biathlon experience, the sport has permeated various aspects of society and popular culture, demonstrating its lasting impact and appeal.

Overall, the sport of biathlon has undeniably left its mark on society and popular culture, transcending its origins as a military training exercise to become a global phenomenon. Its influence can be seen in the values it embodies, the stories it inspires, and the entertainment it provides, solidifying its place as a beloved and impactful sport.

Chapter 13:

Challenges and controversies in biathlon

Biathlon, a sport that combines cross-country skiing and rifle shooting, has faced several challenges and controversies throughout its history. From its military origins to its inclusion in the modern Olympic Games, biathlon has come a long way, but it has not been without its difficulties.

One of the most significant challenges for biathlon has been the use of performance-enhancing drugs. Like many other sports, biathlon has had to contend with athletes who have sought to gain an unfair advantage through the use of banned substances. This has led to several high-profile doping cases and tarnished the reputation of the sport. Biathlon's governing bodies have had to take strong measures to combat the use of performance-enhancing drugs, including implementing strict testing protocols and harsh penalties for those found guilty of doping.

Another controversy that has plagued biathlon is the issue of gender equality. Historically, women have not had the same opportunities as men in many sports, including biathlon. However, in recent years, there has been a push for greater gender equality in the sport, with more opportunities for female athletes and a greater emphasis on women's events. While progress has been made, there is still work to be done to ensure that women have the same opportunities as men in biathlon.

Equipment has also been a source of controversy in biathlon. The sport relies on the use of highly specialized skis, rifles, and other gear, and there have been disputes over the use of technology to gain an unfair advantage. For example, there have been concerns about the use of high-tech rifle sights and other equipment that could give certain athletes an edge over their competitors. Biathlon's governing bodies have had to carefully regulate equipment to ensure a level playing field for all athletes.

Additionally, the sport has faced challenges related to the environment and climate change. Cross-country skiing is heavily dependent on snow, and the changing climate has led to concerns about the viability of biathlon venues in some areas. There have been discussions about the need to adapt the sport to changing environmental conditions, as well as initiatives to make biathlon more sustainable and environmentally-friendly.

Finally, the geopolitics of the sport have also been a source of controversy. Biathlon has deep roots in Eastern Europe, and there have been tensions related to the sport's governance and competition, especially between Russia and other nations. These geopolitical disputes have sometimes spilled over into the competitive arena, leading to heated rivalries and controversies.

Overall, biathlon has faced numerous challenges and controversies throughout its history, but the sport has continued to evolve and thrive in the face of these difficulties. Biathlon's governing bodies have worked to address these issues and ensure the continuing success and growth of the sport. As it progresses into the future, biathlon will continue to face challenges, but its enduring popularity and the dedication of its athletes and fans will ensure that it remains a thrilling and compelling sport for years to come.

Addressing issues such as doping, equipment regulations, and gender equality

Biathlon, a sport with a rich history and a unique combination of cross-country skiing and rifle shooting, has faced numerous challenges and issues over the years. From its military origins to its evolution into an Olympic sport, biathlon has had to address a range of issues, including doping, equipment regulations, and gender equality.

Doping has been a major concern in biathlon, as in many other sports. Athletes using performance-enhancing drugs not only undermine the integrity of the sport but also pose a danger to themselves and others, especially in a sport that involves the use of firearms. Biathlon has implemented strict anti-doping measures, including testing and sanctions for offenders, to ensure fair competition and the health and safety of athletes.

Another issue that biathlon has grappled with is equipment regulations. The sport's combination of skiing and shooting requires specialized gear, and ensuring that all athletes have equal access to high-quality equipment is essential for fair competition. Equipment regulations ensure that all competitors have a level playing field and prevent the use of unfair advantages.

Gender equality has also been a significant issue in biathlon, as in many other sports. Historically, women have faced barriers to participating in sports, and biathlon has not been immune to this challenge. However, the sport has made strides in promoting equality, with women's biathlon events now an established part of the Olympic program and efforts to ensure equal opportunities and support for female athletes.

Overall, biathlon has taken steps to address these and other issues, seeking to uphold the values of fairness, equality, and integrity that are essential for a successful and reputable sport. By addressing these challenges, biathlon has continued to evolve and thrive, proving itself to be a sport worthy of its military origins and its place on the Olympic stage.

Chapter 14:

Future of biathlon as an Olympic sport

Despite its military origins, biathlon has transformed into a highly popular and widely followed sport around the world. The sport has come a long way since the early days of military training exercises, and it has evolved into a modern, dynamic sport that captures the imagination of fans and athletes alike.

While traditionally dominated by European countries, biathlon is now gaining popularity in other parts of the world, particularly in North America and Asia. This increased global interest will lead to a more diverse and competitive field of athletes, ultimately making the sport more exciting and engaging for fans.

Another important aspect of the future of biathlon lies in its potential for technological advancements. The sport has already seen significant developments in equipment and training methods, and these advancements are likely to continue in the coming years. From improvements in rifle technology to advancements in ski materials, these developments will not only improve performance but also attract more interest to the sport.

As a sport that takes place in natural, outdoor settings, biathlon has a vested interest in preserving and protecting the environment. Efforts to minimize the sport's environmental impact, such as reducing energy consumption and carbon emissions, will be crucial in ensuring the sport's continued inclusion in the Olympic program.

Furthermore, the continued success of biathlon as an Olympic sport will depend on the ability of its governing bodies to adapt to changing times and demographics. Efforts to appeal to younger audiences, both as participants and spectators, will be essential in ensuring the long-term sustainability and growth of the sport. This means embracing new forms of media, engaging with fans on social platforms, and creating opportunities for youth involvement in the sport.

As the sport continues to grow and evolve, it has the potential to captivate a global audience and inspire future generations of athletes. With a commitment to sustainability, technological advancement, and inclusivity, biathlon has the potential to remain a highly relevant and exciting Olympic sport for many years to come.

Potential developments and advancements in the sport

The sport of biathlon has a long and storied history, with its roots in military training and survival skills. However, in recent years, the sport has seen significant changes and advancements, which have propelled it into the realm of elite athletic competition. There are several potential developments and advancements that could further elevate the sport of biathlon in the future.

One potential development in the world of biathlon is the continued advancement of equipment and technology. As with many sports, technology has played a crucial role in the evolution of biathlon. From innovative rifles and scopes to cutting-edge ski equipment, the continuous improvement and refinement of equipment have the potential to significantly impact the performance and success of athletes. Advancements in equipment could lead to faster ski times, more accurate shooting, and ultimately, higher levels of competition.

Another potential development in biathlon is the continued expansion and professionalization of the sport. As biathlon continues to gain popularity and recognition on a global scale, there is a growing demand for professional opportunities and infrastructure to support elite athletes. This includes the development of training facilities, coaching programs, and financial support for athletes. As the sport becomes more professionalized, the level of competition is likely to increase, with more athletes vying for success on the world stage.

In addition to advancements in equipment and professionalization, there is also potential for the evolution of the sport itself. This could include changes to the format of competitions, the addition of new events, or modifications to existing rules and regulations. For example, there may be opportunities to introduce new relay formats, mixed-gender events, or team competitions. These changes have the potential to bring more excitement and diversity to the sport, as well as attract new audiences and participants.

Furthermore, the ongoing development of training and coaching methods has the potential to significantly impact the future of biathlon. As our understanding of sports science and human performance continues to advance, there are new opportunities to optimize training programs, improve athletes' physical and mental preparation, and enhance overall performance. This ongoing development has the potential to elevate the level of competition in biathlon, as well as push athletes to achieve new heights of excellence.

From continued improvements in equipment and technology to the expansion and professionalization of the sport, there are many opportunities to take biathlon to new heights. With ongoing dedication and innovation, the future of biathlon looks bright, and the sport is primed for even greater success and recognition on the world stage.

Chapter 15: Conclusion

Reflecting on the evolution of biathlon and its place in the history of winter sports.

Biathlon, a unique combination of cross-country skiing and rifle shooting, has a rich history that dates back to its military roots. Reflecting on the evolution of biathlon and its place in the history of winter sports provides valuable insight into the sport's development and significance.

The earliest known form of biathlon can be traced back to Scandinavia, where early hunters were known to carry rifles while skiing through the snow-covered forests in search of game. This practice of skiing and shooting eventually made its way into military training, as soldiers in countries such as Norway, Sweden, and Finland utilized skiing and marksmanship in their military preparedness.

In the early 20th century, biathlons began to be organized as competitive sporting events. The first recorded biathlon competition took place in 1912 in Trysil, Norway, and consisted of a 17km ski race with four shooting stages. The sport continued to gain popularity, and by the 1930s, biathlon had established itself as a recognized discipline in the Winter Olympics.

Throughout the years, the equipment and techniques used in biathlon have evolved significantly. Early rifles were often single-shot bolt-action models, requiring shooters to reload after each shot. Today, athletes use highly specialized, precision firearms that are specifically designed for biathlon competition. Similarly, the skis and ski bindings have undergone substantial technological advancements, allowing for faster and more efficient movement on the snow.

In addition to equipment, the rules and format of biathlon competitions have also evolved over time. The distance of the ski courses and the number and positioning of shooting stages have been modified to create more dynamic and challenging events. The addition of relay races and mixed relay races have also enhanced the diversity of biathlon competitions, allowing for greater opportunities for athletes to compete and showcase their skills.

From its humble origins as a military exercise to its current status as an esteemed Olympic sport, biathlon has certainly come a long way. Its combination of physical endurance, technical skill, and marksmanship has solidified its place in the history of winter sports. As biathlon continues to evolve and attract new enthusiasts, it will undoubtedly remain a compelling and celebrated discipline in the realm of athletic competition.

Printed in Great Britain
by Amazon